Escape Your Debt

The Ultimate Money Management Guide for Debt Relief

Learn How to Pay off Your Debt
and
Live Debt Free Forever

By
TJ Franklin

2

of the information is without contract or any type of guarantee assurance.

The trademarks that are used are without any consent, and the publication of the trademark is without permission or backing by the trademark owner. All trademarks and brands within this book are for clarifying purposes only and are the owned by the owners themselves, not affiliated with this document.

Table of Contents

Introduction   5

Chapter 1: Why Are You in Debt?   7

Chapter 2: Income and Expense   10
Worksheet

Chapter 3: Can You Raise Your   15
Income?

Chapter 4: Can You Lower Your   19
Expenses?

Chapter 5: Credit Cards and Debt   22

Chapter 6: Debt Consolidation Loans   31

Chapter 7: Bankruptcy   33

Chapter 8: Secured Loans   40

Chapter 9: Anticipate Your   43
Purchases/Expenses

Chapter 10: Staying the Course   46

Conclusion   50

More   52

Introduction

I want to thank you for buying my book, *"Escape Your Debt: The Ultimate Money Management Guide for Debt Relief, Learn How to Pay off Your Debt and Live Debt Free Forever."* This book contains proven steps and strategies on how to pay off your existing debts, and stay debt free for life.

If you're like me, then you have been plagued by your debts long enough, and finally realize it's time to take massive action, and regain control of your financial situation and future. Not long ago, I was in a dire situation where I was drowning in an enormous amount of student loan and credit card debt. I was living paycheck to paycheck, and I was desperate. So I took matters into my own hands. I knew I wanted a better life, and to get there I had to get control of my financial situation. In this book you'll find steps and strategies that can help you pay off your debts and stay financially free forever. These are the same steps and strategies that I have used over the past few years, and have experienced much success with.

There is no get rich quick scheme in this book. No fabulous new cookie cutter way to pay off all your debts overnight. I can't say that I have all the answers for you, but what I do have is a way; a guide to get you to a better place. If you've ended up here reading my book, then you're still searching for a way to that place of financial freedom. It's important to know that this path will take time to travel down, and you will face discouragement, but fear not, because every disciplined effort has multiple rewards. So, if you want a better life, then begin with the choice to do whatever it takes to make it happen.

"Set a goal to become a millionaire for what it will make of you to achieve it."
- Jim Rohn

Chapter 1

Why Are You in Debt?

The first thing you need to ask yourself is, why are you in your current debt situation? At this point, it is best to dedicate a small notebook or a journal for your debt free journey. List down ALL the likely reasons why you are swimming in debt or living from paycheck to paycheck.

To clarify, this is not to shame you. Rather, this is the first step to accepting that you have a problem. It doesn't matter if you spent it for a good cause. For now, just write everything you are spending money on!

For example:

I am using 50% of my income to pay my credit cards.

I bought a cool new tablet PC on installment.

I go out every weekend and party all night.

I've been in the same dead end job for 10 years now.

I am paying for my auto loan.

I am paying for my home mortgage, plus a refinance and a 2nd loan.

I am paying off my student loan.

I pay a lot on utilities, especially for pay per view and cell phone bills.

My rent is too high.

I have alimony payments.

Wants versus Needs

In your list of things, you pay for, what goes to your needs and what goes to your wants? Check the numbers that represent your needs i.e. groceries, alimony, student loan, etc. Also, cross out items that you consider as wants i.e. pay per view, premium cellular phone plans, your new tablet PC.

You Can't Turn Cold Turkey Overnight!

The goal here is to see exactly where you're at with your spending. You'll want to attack your *wants* list first, and start to cut down or eliminate your spending in these areas (I'll talk more about this in Chapter 4).

It is understandable that it is highly unlikely that you will drop all your unnecessary spending in one day. What this exercise is about is making you realize and differentiate between wants and needs.

Chapter 2

Income and Expense Worksheet

An income and expense worksheet allows you to itemize your net monthly income and your total monthly spending. This is essential to knowing why you are in debt. There are downloadable worksheets online. All you need to do is to type the appropriate search words, or you can make your own.

Here's a website with a worksheet template I like to use. It allows you to input your information right into the form and computes everything for you, and then you can either print it out or email it to yourself.

https://counseling.flrministry.com/forms/income_form.asp

If you would like to create your own, then just divide a sheet of paper into two. The left side is dedicated to ALL net income related to your household. Your net income is your gross income minus taxes and any other amount your employer removes with your approval. The right side is dedicated to ALL your expenses.

Monthly I&E

There are those who do not get a monthly paycheck. It is still better to manage the personal financial worksheet on a monthly basis. Add it up to a month or four weeks work of pay. This will allow you to conveniently budget and monitor your monthly spending. By the way, you do not include overtime pay in this worksheet, unless it is something given to you as part of your regular income.

Household Income

If you have a spouse or a family member who shares in all the expenses, then include that amount in the net income. If other household members contribute partially, just add the amount they give. List everything down under household income.

How to Declare Expenses

The right side is where you itemize your expenses. Be as accurate as possible. This means down to the last penny if you have to. In this regard, it is best if you keep receipts from now on. If you are unsure of the amount, make an estimate.

Tip: It is better to give a higher estimate than to under declare the expense.

Miscellaneous and Savings

There will always be little things you cannot account for. Take 10% of your total net income and label it "miscellaneous expenses." At the end of each month, any amount left should be deposited in a savings account. The ideal is to have 5% left.

Amount Due on Credit or Installment

If you are paying for credit cards, or anything else on installment, include the total amount due. Don't declare the minimum! Otherwise you are only paying interest. This runs counter to the way to being debt-free.

It is always best to pay your credit cards in full every month. However, if you have a high revolving balance on your credit cards that you simply cannot pay off with one payment, then you want to pay as much as you can over the minimum. I will discuss in more detail in Chapter 5 on how to handle excessive credit card debt.

The Ideal

After the computation, you want to have 20% to 30% surplus income. This is not including the 10% you declared as miscellaneous. Regardless of how much is left over, the surplus must be deposited to a savings account. This will be your midterm goal. The long-term goal is to save up at least 50% as surplus income.

Here is an example I&E Worksheet

Monthly Income	$	Monthly Expenses	$
Net Income	5,000	Rent	1,000
		Car Payment	250
		Car Insurance	130
		Student Loan	150
		Cable/Internet Package	120
		Cell Phone	80
		Electric	75
		Food	400

Monthly Income	$	Monthly Expenses	$
		Amenities	200
		Entertainment	300
		Gas	250
		Gym	30
		Credit Card Payment	200
		Miscellaneous Expenses	500
TOTAL	5,000	TOTAL	3,685
Surplus Income (26%)	1,315		

Chapter 3

Can You Raise Your Income?

Let's look at some ways you can generate more income. Apart from cutting down your expenses, increasing your income is another way to help pay down your debts faster. Ask yourself these questions: "Is this the best that I can do?" "Is this the most income I can take home? "How can I increase my income?" Find out ways through which you can add another stream of income. Here are a few suggestions.

Getting a Raise

How's your performance at work? Most companies have a semiannual and annual performance assessment. If you think your work is above average, then you should ask for a raise. How much should you ask? The standard is 5% to 10%, depending on your performance and the profits generated by the company.

Ask Through Formal Channels

Before that, review the company policy. This way you know you are not stepping on anyone's toes. Send out a memo to your H.R., cite procedure and state your performance. End it with a note saying, you are willing to do a sit down.

Increasing Profits

If you are a businessperson, then your profits and losses rest on your shoulders. How's business been lately? The key to generating profits is two things:

First, your product must have value. Value means, something that does what it is supposed to do, and then some! Remember, it is not about lowering your sticker price. It is about giving consumers what they want and doing it better than the competition.

Second, your product must be relevant. This means something that people want. The best sellers are those who generate relevance, not wait on it. If your product is new, then make it known. Make people want it. If it's old, find ways to bring it back into circulation. If you're struggling with this, consider getting a business mentor or coach. This will cost money upfront, but in the long run, your business will grow and generate more income.

Second Job

Nowadays, finding a second job is not really a problem. There are many online home-based jobs out there. These opportunities allow you to stay at home but still make decent money. Tip: find the job that suits you best. A few of the most popular online jobs are:

Selling stuff (eBay, Craigslist, Facebook, etc.)
Content writing
Transcription services
Web development and maintenance
Search engine optimization
Coaching/online tutors

A New Job

If your job is a dead end, maybe it's time for you to move on. A dead end job is one that does not provide you with personal and professional growth. It is also one with a toxic environment that drains all your energy.

Nowadays, most job applications are electronic and can be accessed directly from the company's website. There is also a host of online job listing sites. Most of these sites will let you refine your searches to specifics, and setup daily or weekly email notifications of jobs that match your search criteria. Make it a point to dedicate at least 15 minutes a night to your job hunting.

Tip: don't resign until you've found something else first. If you choose to stay at your current job, now you should have more guts to demand higher pay. In any case, you still have your current job as a fall back.

Chapter 4

Can You Lower Your Expenses?

This is something you do, regardless if you get a raise, and/or a part-time job. The question is "how low can you go?" Below are a few points you want to consider.

"Premium" Debt Traps

If you see the word "premium" or any word of similar import, attached to a utility bill, then you are paying too much. Popular examples are cable, Internet connectivity, cellular phone providers, etc. Your goal is to save money! So go back to basic plans.

Tip: Be careful with bundled plans. The only time you apply for one is if you actually need everything in the bundle. At the very least you want to pay less per month, than if you applied for a separate plan. If you need only two out of three, and it ends up costing more, then separate plans is better.

Postpaid versus Prepaid

You need to identify what to pay for monthly and pay for "per use." For example, do you really need a postpaid cellular phone? Will a prepaid phone kit suit your personality better? This way you can minimize the calls you make. Besides, texting is cheaper.

Eating Out versus Cooking

Eating out or ordering take out is convenient, but it is more expensive in many ways. First, you can cut your food allowance by half if you cook your own meals. Second, you eat healthier and can control your diet better. This minimizes the risk of you getting hospitalized, developing health issues, or needing expensive medicines.

Electricity

How about lowering your use of air conditioning or heating? Don't leave your appliances, especially your TV on all the time. Most experts believe that proper use of electricity can lower your bills quarter to half every month. While you're at it, one by one, change your expensive light bulbs into fluorescent, or better yet, switch to LED, they're both much more efficient.

Fashionably Broke

Do you really need another pair of signature brand jeans? Does your one-year-old phone really need replacing? Chances are the answer is, NO.

Tip: If you have a change of clothes for two weeks, plus several party essentials, that's good enough. Unless your phone breaks, don't buy a new one.

Your motto should be: live simply.

Chapter 5

Credit Cards and Debt

In today's economy, everybody needs a credit card. The problem is, most consumers have no idea what a credit card is for. They think that it is a means to spend more than what they earn. In reality, credit cards are supposed to provide convenience for those who can afford to spend money.

Statistically speaking, consumers in their mid 20s to mid 30s have an average of five to seven credit cards per person. That's just too many! Realistically speaking you only need two or three cards. One should be tied up to a savings or current account. The other is an Internet purchase card. The third is kept on reserve for big-ticket purchases on installment.

The General Rule

If you cannot afford to pay the full amount credited for your necessities on a single month, then you are over charging. For big-ticket purchases i.e. a new laptop, LED TV, washing machine, etc., if you cannot get it on zero installment and pay for it in three to six months, then you cannot afford it. This is assuming you have thought carefully about the purchase. For big-ticket purchases, it is best to pay them off one at a time.

Minimum Payment

This means you are paying for the interest only. This is a bad idea. You're probably thinking, "I'll just pay for it next month." The problem is, next month there will be another set of charges. If you can't pay for this month, then stop charging! Pay off all your credit card debts first. For now, use cash.

How Many Cards Should I Have?

In my early research, I quickly adopted the assumption that you should have no more than three cards, and should pay off and close any additional accounts. However, the more I dug the more I found conflicting information on this subject matter. Here's what I believe and what I have found to work best for me.

Ideally, you should have a minimum of three cards, no more than five. If you have more than five, don't panic, simply work on paying off the other cards, and then leave them alone and inactive, but don't close them.

Here's why; a big part of your credit score is based on the number of cards you have. If you have too little (two or less) the credit bureaus will not have enough information on you to know how responsible you are. If you have too many cards (more than five) then the credit bureaus may ping you as more of a liability because you can dig yourself into an enormous amount of debt. Having three to five cards will give them just enough information about your spending habits and payment history to make an informed decision.

Closing accounts may lower your score because it's partial based on the average length of your accounts; therefore, if you close accounts you risk the chance of lowering the average age of your accounts, and the younger your account history is, the lower your score will be. If you feel like you will be tempted to keep using all your cards then just cut up the cards to the extra account, but don't officially close the accounts.

Tip: Keep using the cards with the most use, best redemption value, and the longest positive account history.

If you cannot pay all of your credit cards off at once, then your best option is to start with the card or cards that have the highest interest rate regardless of the total amount due. Pay them off first because these cards will cost you the most money in the long run. You may have to pay off one card at a time.

It's also not a good idea to open up retail store credit cards, for the simple fact that this card limits you to only the one store, and the interest alone will far exceed the small percentage you save by using the card. Since you will only be keeping three to five cards on hand for purchases you don't want one of them to be limited to only one store. It's best to have revolving accounts with major credit cards, i.e., Visa, MasterCard, American Express, and Discover.

Other Strategies

Don't expect this to happen overnight. This process will take time; quite possibly years. The most important thing is to stick with your game plan.

You may find that you're not even able to pay off one card at a time, and you're only able to make the minimum payment on each card. Choose one card to work on paying off first.

Again, ideally you want to choose the card with the highest interest rate. Start paying more then the minimum on this one card. It doesn't matter how much more, $5, $10, $20; you just want to get the ball rolling. Pay however much more you can whenever you can. If you come into extra money, such as an income tax refund, or you worked some overtime hours at your job, use that money to pay down your balance even more. You might not like this, and your budget will be tight for a while, but you have to discipline yourself and stay proactive.

Once you have paid off this one credit card, then take the minimum that you were paying and apply it to another card. For example, let's say you were paying $25 a month on the card you just paid off, and the next card you are going to start paying off has a minimum payment of $20 a month. Simply start paying $45 a month on this card. This is the way your debts will start to get paid off faster. Don't just pocket the $25 because you no longer have a balance on that card because that's counterproductive to what you're trying to accomplish here. You may be paying a higher minimum, but, in essence, your total monthly expenses are essentially the same. Stay the course and you will see results.

One Caveat

Some of you may find that you're becoming discouraged because you're slowly paying off a rather *large* outstanding balance on your credit card, and it can make you feel very stagnant. I will say again, it is always best to pay off the credit card or cards with the highest interest rate first; however, if that card is carrying a large, like in the thousands, balance and you're paying only a small amount each month towards the balance, then it can take years to pay off. You may begin to feel like progress is not being made and give up. Don't give up. At this point, I would suggest you choose the credit card with the lowest total balance regardless of the interest rate. Go ahead and pay this card off first. It's important to build momentum and keep yourself motivated. There's no point in paying a card with a large balance and high interest if it's going to knock you out of the box. Paying off credit cards with smaller balances will happen faster and make you feel like you're making progress. **The most important thing is to get to the end result - debt free.**

Credit Counseling and Consolidation Services

You may have seen the commercials and heard the ads for credit counseling and consolidation services. Honestly, you really don't need these guys. Most are a scam; some are legit, but anything they can do, you can do yourself with a little legwork. They usually charge a fee for their services, and are really just become the middleman between you and your creditors.

The Federal Trade Commission has some good information on their website about dealing with these services, credit cards and debt. Here's the website address to their page:

http://www.consumer.ftc.gov/topics/dealing-debt

Additional Tips

I've spent much time over the years learning about credit card companies and how they report their information to the credit bureaus (Experian, Equifax and TransUnion). Here are some additional tips about how to manage your credit cards so they reflect favorably upon your credit report.

1. 30% of your credit score is based on your percentage of debt in relation to the limit. For example, say you have a credit card with a limit of $1,000 and you have charged $200 worth of purchases, then your debt to limit ratio is 20%. Ideally, you want this ratio to never go higher than 30%.

2. It's a good idea to periodically check to make sure your credit card companies are reporting the correct credit limit of your cards to the credit bureaus. Many times they will report an incorrect limit amount, usually one that is less than your actual limit, which the credit bureaus have no way of knowing is wrong. This is bad. First, it changes the debt to limit ratio to a less than favorable percentage that could lower your overall credit score. Second, the lower your overall credit score is the higher your interest rates will be.

3. Ask for a credit limit increase. Some credit card companies will allow you to do this right online from your account. I would suggest trying this once every six months. An increase in your credit limit will help to lower your debt to credit limit ratio. If you do choose to go this route, don't be foolish and use the new increase in credit.

4. Ask for a lower interest rate. You'd be surprised what credit card companies are willing to do to keep your business. They may have to run your credit report, but a lower interest rate would mean less money out of your pocket in the long run. You may even be able to take advantage of new promotions or balance transfers with 0% APR. If you can get approved for one of these deals, then you can transfer the balance from one of your other cards with a high interest rate.

Chapter 6

Debt Consolidation Loans

A debt consolidation loan is a financial instrument to get out of debt. A consumer, who has several overdue debts, applies for a loan, the total amount of which is used to pay all or a substantial portion of his debts. This agreement can be with any of the debtor's existing creditors or a new creditor.

Some so-called experts argue that leaving small debts alone is better. This is because small time creditors cannot report the debt to a credit bureau. These so called experts would rather that you concentrate on paying credit card debts by way of balance transfer or debt to loan conversion. What these geniuses don't realize is that, small debts can be sold to collection agencies! If a collection agency reports a debt, then it becomes many times worse than an overdue credit card debt.

The Parameters

Debt consolidation should be done after due diligence, and knowing the consequences. In order for it to work, you need to have specific requirements. These are:

> You need to pay for the whole, or at least a substantial portion of your overdue, and interest earning debts.

> The average interest on all the debts to be paid is higher than the consolidation loan interest rate.

> The interest rate must be fixed.

> You need a source of regular income, and surplus income at that!

> Put a temporary and 100% stop on buying "wants." At least after you have paid of ALL your overdue debts.

My Credit Rating

On most loans, you want to have excellent credit scores. On a consolidation loan, you can make do with above median scores. This is because you want to stop your debtors from reporting your debts to credit bureaus. What if you have below median credit scores? Then chances are you cannot afford a consolidation loan. In which case you have to consider other alternatives.

Chapter 7

Bankruptcy

If you cannot afford to pay your debts, in full or on installment, then you have two options:

First, you can disregard the debt. This is easy, but the problem will not go away. It will only get worst. Your debts will pile up and when you do need to get a car loan, home loan, personal loan, etc., you will be denied the facility of credit.

Second, you can file for bankruptcy. Even if it may not seem like a viable option to get out of debt, it would be a good idea to keep an open mind, and read on.

Total Liquidation

The popular misconception is that, bankruptcy will wipe away all your debts and all of your properties. This cannot be farther from the truth. First, as a general rule, only unsecured debts will be subjected to bankruptcy proceedings. Second, the filer can request to have certain properties exempted. These usually comprise of a reasonably priced home, necessities, items needed to make a living i.e.

tools of a trade, professional library, etc. Think about it, credit card debts are unsecured. Most personal loans are also unsecured.

Payment Plan

In some cases, the court will decree that you should pay your debts, albeit only partially. This usually happens if the bankruptcy filer has the capacity to make partial payments and it is only the hard headedness of creditors that prevents it.

The court will supervise a payment plan to be approved by creditors. If the creditors object too vehemently, the court may actually rule for a payment plan less favorable to them.

If this happens you get to keep more property, but you still end up paying on installment. This is just like a consolidation loan, but only more advantageous to you.

Chapter 7, Chapter 11, or Chapter 13?

You'll have to decide which bankruptcy chapter is best for you. A Chapter 7 bankruptcy is what's known as a liquidation bankruptcy and will wipe out your unsecured debts such as medical bills and credit cards. This chapter also requires that you have little or no disposable income.

Chapter 11 bankruptcy is for businesses mainly a partnership or limited liability company, and allows for the reorganization of finances through modify payment terms.

Chapter 13 bankruptcy is more commonly used when someone has a regular income and can pay back their debts, and have a significant amount of equity in their home, or property that they would like to keep.

The United States Courts website has some good additional information about the basics of bankruptcy. Here is their wed address:

http://www.uscourts.gov/FederalCourts/Bankruptcy.aspx

Tip: Be sure to check with your state as well for any specific filing requirements.

What About My Credit Rating?

As mentioned earlier, bankruptcy is a last resort. Yes, it is true that your credit score will probably end up "poor" after you get discharged from your debt, but realistically speaking, your score is already shot because of the many defaults that led up to you seriously considering bankruptcy.

The bankruptcy discharge will remain on your report for 7 to 10 years; however, you can always rebuild your credit before then. Current activity weighs the heaviest. Don't leave your credit stagnant. Start to rebuild right away. There are many resources out there that can guide you on this. In which case, you can eventually raise your credit score to excellent. In the meantime, lenders will still be reluctant to grant you a loan. That doesn't mean no one will loan to you. It will be harder, but you have a better chance getting loan approval with a previous bankruptcy discharge, than with a debt ridden credit report that spanned a couple, or even several years.

Note: It is difficult to remove a bankruptcy from your credit report prior to the 7 to 10 year marker. There are credit repair companies that claim they can do this; however, according to the Federal Trade Commission it is illegal to remove accurate negative information from a credit file. If you find a third party company that can do this for you, it is likely that after sometime the bankruptcy will reappear on your credit report.

Rebuilding Your Credit

If you are in the process of rebuilding your credit, then it's best to apply for secured credit cards. Secured credit cards differ from regular credit cards because they offer you a line a credit that is secured by an amount of funds you must first deposit into a collateral bank account. For example, let's say you deposit $200 into your collateral account, and then your credit limit on your secured credit card will be $200. When you use your card you will be billed monthly for the balance. The money will not be automatically taken from your collateral account; therefore, you must make the payments each month. The collateral account is there in case you default on your payments.

Tip: Make sure you pay every single bill on time from here on out. You do not want to miss or make any late payments while you're in the process of rebuilding your credit.

Tip: If you're married, you and your spouse should apply for new credit separately.

Here are some secured credit cards to help you rebuild your credit that are highly recommended for those whose credit scores are below 550:

First Progress Platinum Prestige

First Progress Platinum Elite

First Progress Platinum Select

Open Sky

Merrick Bank Secured Visa

Tip: You can find additional information and credit card suggestions at www.creditcard.com

Your Credit Report

You are entitled to a free credit report from all three of the major credit bureaus (Equifax, Experian, TransUnion) every 12 months. However, ideally, you want to check your credit report every four months. You can easily purchase your credit report with or without the score directly from the website of each of the credit bureaus.

Note: Your credit report will usually only be available for 30 days unless you subscribe to a service that provides year around access.

Here is the website where you can request your annual free credit reports:

https://www.annualcreditreport.com/index.action

Reporting Discrepancies

When reviewing your credit reports you may find some discrepancies. It's fairly easy to dispute these right on the website for each of the credit bureaus. I recommend doing this for any information you find that is questionable.

Note: Creditors are required to report to the credit bureaus every month.

Here are the website addresses to the three major credit bureaus:

http://www.equifax.com/

http://www.experian.com/

http://www.transunion.com/

Chapter 8

Secured Loans

These are midterm to long-term loans that have a mortgage clause i.e. home loan, auto loan, business loan, etc. This means you promise to pay the loan, under threat of foreclosure of the collateral. The collateral can be property, which was bought from the proceeds of the loan, and/or a different property. They sometimes can carry a lower interest rate because the bank can collect the collateral if you default on your payments.

Opportunity versus Risk

You need to weigh the pros and cons of taking out a long-term loan versus not doing so. Yes, it is a debt, but if it means:

Buying a home of your own, at a reasonable price, as opposed to renting a property within the same price range, then maybe it is worth the risk.

Being able to go to and from work more conveniently at an affordable rate. Why not!

Getting your hands on more money to invest wisely. Take the risk!

It is not a good idea to transfer your unsecured debt (credit cards, medical bills, etc.) to a secured loan. If you try this, let's say, by taking a second mortgage out on your home, then you risk putting your home in jeopardy should you default on the payments.

Important Points to Remember

Don't allow yourself to get your hands on the money itself. Take out a loan to be directly paid to the realtor or dealer. Have the check paid out to the business name. This way you avoid the temptation of misspending.

Only take out a long-term loan if your credit rating is excellent. This way you get the lowest interest rates and the best loan terms. Only accept fixed interest rates. The payment period should be long enough to be manageable but not too long that your total interest payments become too high. As a general rule, you want ALL your monthly loans and installment payments NOT to exceed 30% of your monthly net income.

Tip: Your bank is a good place to start when looking for secured loans. You may qualify for a better rate since you already have an established history with them.

Chapter 9

Anticipate Your
Purchases/Expenses

Even the most frugal consumers fall victim to this. Always anticipate the cost of maintenance and the average life span of every item you own and use. This is especially true for big-ticket items like your car, laptop, washing machine, stovetop, air conditioner and/or heater, etc. This way you save up for the eventual purchase.

You also save up for emergencies. Of course, you do not want something bad to happen, but it is better to have a nest egg for this sort of thing. If you and your family members are prone to medical preconditions that require expensive hospitalization, then make sure your medical plan is properly configured. It might not be a bad idea to apply for health insurance as well. While you are at it, make sure you have sufficient dental coverage.

Buy Used

If you can, buy used items. Of course there are certain things you want to buy brand new. As a general rule, used items are 25% to 50%

cheaper. Do your research. There are plenty of high quality goods that are sold second hand. Sometimes these are even better than what you can buy brand new, within your budget. Examples of used items to buy are:

House and/or lot
Automobile
Wooden furniture (pure wood, not particle board)
Automatic watches
Books
Signature T-shirts, jeans, jackets, etc., (garage sale)

Examples of items you DO NOT buy second hand:

Underwear
Electronic devices that are out of warranty i.e. laptop, cellular phone, TV
Footwear
Children's toy
Any item for an infant

Consider shopping online. You can usually find the same designer items for less even after factoring in shipping. Also, make sure to visit the websites of every department store before shopping there because they sometimes offer coupons for additional savings that you can print out and bring into the store.

Examples of some trust worthy online sites are:

Amazon
ebay
Overstock.com

In Bulk or Per Piece?

If you do need to make purchases, you need to determine if you should buy it all at the same time or one at a time. How much money can you spare? If you can do it once, chances are it will be cheaper. Consider your transportation expense. If you regularly go there anyway, then you have the option of staggered buying.

Tip: Anticipate regular times of the year when an item you absolutely need will go on sale.

Remember, you buy on sale items you will need. You do not buy items you may need because there is a sale.

Chapter 10

Staying the Course

If you've come this far, don't drop the ball now. If you want to stay debt free then you need to continue down the path you've created with the help of this book. Make it a point to stay on top of your finances. Make smart decisions about your spending; invest wisely and for the long term, and do away with all limiting beliefs about money. Stay healthy and positive, both physically and mentally. Below are several reasons why this is relevant to your financial freedom!

Healthy Body, Healthy Mind

Ask any physician, dietician, or even your mom! If you keep your body in tiptop shape, then your brain will follow. Simply put, your mind is part of your body. If you want it to work right, you better start treating it right. Develop positive empowering affirmations to feed yourself daily. Meditate.

Healthy Attitude

Let go of any negative mindset you have about money. You cannot become debt free if all you do is think about your debts. Erase the word *debt* from your vocabulary; replace it with the word *progress*. Think about it, if you're paying off your debts then you are making progress, so instead of you making a list of your monthly expenses, make it a list of your monthly progress. Think prosperity. Focus on how your life will be once you are financially free. Imagine it, feel it, live it!

Healthy Diet

As mentioned earlier, it is better to eat home cooked meals than to eat out. Take things one step further and go organic. Eat more greens, leafy greens, fruits, nuts, and the like. Eat less carbs and less sugar, minimize the intake of fatty meats, and stop buying junk food and sugary drinks. Buy a juicer. Eat smaller portion meals at least 6x a day. Don't skip meals. This will only lead to you over eating after.

Exercise

The least you should do is 10,000 steps a day. Buy a pedometer. That will cost you $10 to $20. That should help you keep accurate track of your steps per day. Take up healthy hobbies like jogging, swimming, biking, etc. Do it for 20 to 30 minutes two to four times a week. Join a gym; it will be one of the best investments you ever make for yourself, provided that you go. Check out YouTube for simple easy to follow fitness routines that you can do right in your own home. Exercising regularly has a host of health benefits.

Sleep

Adults need at least six hours uninterrupted sleep every day. For good measure, try to get eight hours. If you can sneak a short 30-minute nap in the afternoon, all the better! You might think this is time wasted, but most experts agree that an afternoon nap allows you to think faster and move better. A faster thinker is one who works smarter!

Get Regular Check Ups

At the very least, you want to have an annual physical, twice a year if possible. This way your physician catches anything before it gets serious. In medical terms, serious is synonymous to expensive. Although, the more you take care of your mind and body, the less you'll have to go to the doctor, and the longer you'll be around to enjoy your financial freedom.

Love Yourself

Invest in you. Find balance in all areas of your life, and eliminate all things that don't allow you to grow. There is abundance all around us, and you deserve to have it. Chase your dreams, believe it can happen, and make it become your reality.

Conclusion

Thank you again for buying my book! If you enjoyed it, and it has made a difference for you, please take the time to share your thoughts by posting a review on the site you bought this book from, I would greatly appreciate it! If it didn't meet your expectations, then let me know your suggests for improvements.

I hope this book was able to help you get control of your financial situation and move you towards a debt free future for life.

The next step is to take your newfound knowledge and apply it to your life for the rest of your life. By applying the methods in this book coupled with a positive and healthy attitude towards money, you're sure to set yourself on the right track.

Enjoy the process and make the commitment to be financially free.

Dream Believe & Become!

Thank you and good luck!

TJ Franklin

P.S. Check out my blog for more great resources to change your life.

www.ChangeYourLifedbb.com

Check Out My Other Books on Amazon

3 Sixty Five: Your Everyday Guide to 365 Inspirational Quotes to Live By

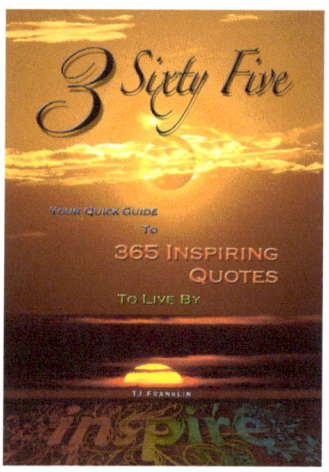

A collection of 365 inspirational quotes, and some of the best advice from the greatest philosophers, authors, influential figures and foremost thinkers of our time. Learn the secrets to success, life, love, happiness, and fruitful longevity.

The Sum of All Thoughts: A Collection of Poetry and Spoken Word Memoirs

This book is a collection of poetry and spoken word memoirs that detail my thoughts, feelings, and actions towards people and experiences that moved me to emotional depths I didn't understand, nor could explain, until I finally put a pen to paper, and unleashed the harbored emotions that held me at bay from a nurturing life.

www.ingramcontent.com/pod-product-compliance
Lightning Source LLC
Chambersburg PA
CBHW040918180526
45159CB00002BA/520